Sir Walter

Chapter 5
Lesson 83: More Digraphs
Lexile® Measure: 620L

ISBN 978-1-62382-039-8

Walter wants to be a knight just like his father, Sir Knox. Walter's mother is Lady Zelda. They live in an English manor on a grassy knoll in Knottington.

Walter is 12 years old. He has only one more year until he can work for the Duke of Knottington. The duke's name is Lord Wraith.

When Walter turned six years old, he began the first phase of becoming a knight. During this time, his mother and father taught him many things.

His mother taught him to be polite to his elders. She taught him to have good table manners. His mother also taught him how to write the alphabet and how to read. She taught him to know right from wrong.

His father taught him how to clean the stable and to care for animals. He taught Walter how to hunt and fish. He also taught Walter how to clean and take care of armor.

Soon, Walter will begin the next phase of becoming a knight. He will be a squire for Lord Wraith. There, he will learn the skills of a knight. Walter will learn the knack of riding horses while dressed in armor. He will trade in his small knife for a large, shiny sword. Walter will learn how to direct a long sword with a turn of his wrist. He will learn how to protect himself and his country.

After a few years of being a "knight in training," Walter will attend a ceremony. At the ceremony, he will become a real knight. He will kneel and promise to always defend a lady. He will promise to speak only the truth. He will promise to be true to the king and to be devoted to the church. He will also promise to defend the helpless. Walter will be brave. Knights never run from danger because of fear.

After the ceremony, Walter will be assigned to protect the king. He will get his own sword. He will get armor knit with metal chains. He will also get a cloak to wrap around his shoulders. The cloak will have a crest on it. The crest is designed to represent the king. People will call Walter "Sir Walter" because he will be a real knight.

The End

Comprehension Questions

1. This passage is about
    a. how Walter will become a knight.
    b. a famous knight named Sir Walter.
    c. how Sir Walter battled an evil dragon.

2. Walter's father
    a. is the king.
    b. is a knight.
    c. died in a battle.

3. Walter will attend a ceremony to become a knight. Which of the following is NOT a time to have a *ceremony*?
    a. when someone gets married
    b. when someone graduates from school
    c. when someone finishes his/her homework

4. If a knight saw a big dragon that was about to eat a child, he would probably

   a. run away.

   b. call the police.

   c. fight to save the child.

5. As part of Walter's training, he learned to

   a. use a light saber.

   b. speak like a dragon.

   c. clean and take care of armor.

Skill Words

alphabet	knife	Knox	write*
assigned	knight	phase	wrong
designed	knit	Wraith	
knack	knoll	wrap	
kneel	Knottington	wrist	

Most Common Words

a	has	of	when
after	have	old	while
also	he	on	will
always	him	one	with
an	his	only	work
and	how	own	write*
animals	in	people	year
around	is	right	years
at	it	run	
be	just	she	
being	know	small	
because	large	soon	
call	learn	the	
can	like	there	
country	live	they	
father	long	things	
few	many	this	
first	more	time	
for	mother	to	
from	name	turn	
get	never	turns	
good	next	wants	

Challenge Words

becoming	metal	shoulder	taught
danger	promise	shoulders	truth
manor	represent	sword	

*both Skill Word and Most Common Word